HOW TO WORK WITH YOUR LAWYER

HOW TO WORK WITH YOUR LAWYER

Book One: The Law in Six Minutes™ Series

Short Books Examining the Law and Legal System
In Terms a Non Lawyer Can Understand

Bryan M. Dench, Esq.

ISBN-13: 9781523317301
ISBN-10: 1523317302
Library of Congress Control Number: 2016900495
CreateSpace Independent Publishing Platform
North Charleston, South Carolina

Introduction to The Law in Six Minutes™ Series

Why have I called this series "The Law in Six Minutes™ "?

My good wife, who is much cleverer than I when it comes to presentation and marketing of ideas, suggested calling this, "If talk is cheap, why does it cost so much to talk to my lawyer?" Clearly she was on to something, as lawyers' services can be very expensive and most people *think* they are very expensive, if not too expensive.

I'm aware of the cynicism addressed toward lawyers by many people. I've heard all the "lawyer jokes." I know there are people who dislike lawyers in general, except maybe for the one they need when they have a problem or are in trouble of some kind.

But I didn't take the suggestion because I don't want to reinforce the prejudice, especially when failing to get proper legal advice can lead to very unfortunate, if not disastrous, consequences for individuals, families, and businesses. I stuck with a title that suggests short sprints of time to read, and that relates to the life of the practicing lawyer, who must learn to reckon time in an unusual way.

Normal people don't think in six-minute blocks of time. We think of things like, "Oh, that'll take five minutes." Or, "I'll be over in fifteen minutes." You would think somebody odd who said, "Sure, I can come right over. I'll be there in 18 minutes." If your friend asked you how long it would take to mail a letter for him, would you say, "No problem, that will only take six minutes"? No, of course you wouldn't.

Lawyers are different. Once you get out of law school and take a job with a law firm, or even open your own practice under a shingle you hang out, you have to learn to change the way you think about time. You have to start to think in six-minute intervals. Why? Because most of a lawyer's work is charged for by the hour and broken down into tenths of an hour. An hour is sixty minutes, so one tenth is . . . six minutes.

When I started practicing law many years ago, it was hard to get used to thinking of my work in terms of six minute blocks of time. After a while it gets to be second nature, but the lawyer's typical standard unit to measure his or her productivity is the six minute interval. As Abraham Lincoln said, a lawyer's time and advice are his stock in trade, and so in a way it's units of time that lawyers sell.

Of course that time is only valuable if the advice you get in that time is worthwhile. Naturally you want to be sure any lawyer you consult knows his or her stuff. It may be well worth it to pay more for experience and expertise. Part of becoming a good lawyer is gaining experience actually handling legal matters. That's really the only way to learn. Smarts and hard work can make up for a lot in the experience department, but not everything. The best lawyer to consult is one with knowledge and plenty of concrete experience handling the kind of problem that you have or tasks like the one you need accomplished.

Then how efficient and effective will the lawyer be in those precious six-minute slices of time while you're paying the lawyer for advice? That depends a lot on the lawyer's ability to communicate. If you sit through a one hour consultation with a lawyer, which could cost you $400, you would like to be able to communicate with that lawyer, right? Well, there's a problem.

Many lawyers are not very good communicators. Law school doesn't teach you to communicate with normal human beings. It teaches you to think clearly and quickly. It teaches you to survive ridicule and to survive under pressure. It teaches you how to communicate in legal and technical terminology. These are all things you need to know. But do they help you to communicate effectively with your clients, people without legal training? No.

After someone survives three years of law school, there is a terrible temptation for him to believe himself intellectually superior to others. The lawyer, by training, tends to be analyzing a problem as he hears it and thinking of solutions, THE solution. This presents a danger of jumping to a conclusion too soon, before hearing the client out, and as a result imposing the solution on the client rather than developing the solution with the client.

Lawyers aren't always good listeners. And there is an almost irresistible impulse to use the complex and specialized vocabulary of the law in every discussion, even with people who simply cannot be expected to understand it. You worked so hard and suffered so much to acquire that learning; you just have to show it off.

So does this contribute to effective communication between you and your lawyer? No, it doesn't. You might come out of your meeting, paying for your total of six-minute increments, without learning or understanding all that you might.

Over the years I have been privileged to meet with and advise thousands of people. One thing many of them have told me is that they had a hard time understanding the other lawyers they talked to, but that they can understand me. I'm very grateful for that. If it's true I have been able to communicate well with people, I am humbled by that and hope I can continue and get better at it in the years to come.

This is what gave me the idea for "The Law in Six Minutes™" books.

Sitting and talking to clients I spend a good deal of time trying to explain complicated legal matters in terms that will be easy for them to understand and that will make them feel confident they know what they're doing in their legal affairs. And why not? They should be able to understand. These problems are often not that complicated. They just are not known to non-lawyers.

Lawyers are not smarter than other people, no matter what we might think. We just have training and (let's hope) experience others do not. Our job should be to use that to help people and to do it in a way that the people we are trying to help understand and have the ability to participate meaningfully in solving the problems.

Some lawyers don't even try. I have seen lawyers gloss over parts of a problem rather than try to explain what they are doing or why. I have seen some times when lawyers don't even try to explain. There could be a number of reasons. Some clients, though very few, just don't want things explained. When that happens I think we should still try.

Sometimes lawyers are just in too much of a hurry or don't want to bother to explain. That is inexcusable. Some lawyers I fear don't really have a good enough command of what they are doing to explain it. In some cases, the lawyer may fear that the client will not understand or will be overwhelmed. That's possible, but this just means the lawyer needs to make more of an effort to explain clearly and effectively.

The purpose of this series of short, simple books on legal subjects is to help close the communications gap. The idea is that no matter how complicated, it should be possible to give at least an adequate basic explanation of any legal concept in six minutes. Each book looks at one legal subject, say the law of leases, and gives explanations of the basic principles in sections that would take six minutes or less to read and understand.

If you read one of those self-help books it can be helpful to you but also can be dangerous. They can make people think they can solve their own legal problem without a lawyer. That's a big mistake.

Some of the books are hundreds of pages of in-depth discussions that, while maybe a help, are probably too much to digest helpfully.

The idea of "The Law in Six Minutes™" books is not to replace the advice of a capable lawyer. It's to help you get more value from the advice of your lawyer because you can understand things better. I hope these books will also be helpful to you after you consult your lawyer, as a way to go back over things your lawyer has told you to deepen your understanding.

These books are written to be easy for anyone to read. "The Law in Six Minutes™" series won't replace your lawyer's advice but will help you get more value from it because you can understand things better. I hope these books will also be helpful to you after you consult your lawyer as a way to go back over things your lawyer has told you to deepen your understanding of your discussion.

In short, I'm not aiming to replace your lawyer and certainly not suggesting you should try to act as your own lawyer. I'm trying to help you use your lawyer more cost effectively. I want you to feel more confident about the advice you get because you understand it, and because reading these books might help you to ask the right questions of your lawyer.

I've also included a glossary of terms in each book. If you read one of "The Law in Six Minutes™" books and want to know more, you'll find no shortage of longer and more complicated books to read.

Bryan M. Dench
Falmouth, Maine
January 2016

DISCLAIMER

A book written by a lawyer couldn't be complete without some legalese; the best legalese is a disclaimer. This is a disclaimer. A disclaimer is aimed at telling you what you cannot count on. This one is to make sure that you understand that this book is a simplified version of legal terms and concepts that are much more complicated in reality, that are applied by courts and others in the legal system who would not and should not give this book any weight as a legal authority. So just because you read it here does not mean a court or other legal authority will agree to any claim or action you want to take based on the information that's here. I have made every effort to give you accurate and clear information, but reading this is not to be relied on as legal advice or as a substitute for qualified legal representation and advice.

The Law in Six Minutes™ Series

E ach book is designed as an easy read for busy people, a concise summary of a specific body of law, aimed at being readable by a lay person. This will enable the reader to understand the general legal principles and help the reader to prepare better to work with his or her lawyer. I've tried also to break each one down into short segments that could be read in about six minutes.

Bryan Dench, Esquire, is a graduate of Harvard College and the University of Maine School of Law. Chairman of the board of the law firm of Skelton, Taintor and Abbott, Bryan has over forty years of results representing and advising businesses, governmental entities and individuals in complex commercial and regulatory affairs, estate planning, trust and tax matters, mergers and acquisitions, municipal and educational administrative proceedings, mediations, and labor negotiations. He has a Martindale-Hubbell AV Peer rating (highest rating), is a Fellow, American College of Trust and Estate Counsel (ACTEC) and listed in Best Lawyers in America, The Best of the U.S. List of the Best Lawyers and Super Lawyers°. During his long and distinguished legal career, Bryan also served on the court appointed body that administers ethics discipline to lawyers and has testified as an expert among other things on legal ethics and professional responsibility.

Bryan has worked with thousands of people, advising and counseling them through difficult and stressful experiences, such as divorce, death of a family member, lawsuits, criminal defense, tax audits and disputes, labor negotiations, and high stakes business negotiations. Bryan has also served many times as a mediator in legal disputes, bringing to bear skills in problem solving and working through difficult impasses.

In this series Bryan will share with the reader insights based on this long experience and will communicate, in accessible language, the basics of important legal subjects many of us encounter from day to day.

The Law in Six Minutes™
Book One: How to Work
With a Lawyer

Some of us deal with lawyers and legal matters all the time, and find it comfortable (even enjoyable) to work with lawyers and talk to them. However, that's not true for most people.

For most of us encounters with lawyers, legal matters, and the legal system are rare and often unpleasant or intimidating. Even appearing in court on a relatively routine and minor traffic offense can make the best of us anxious. Going through a divorce or other family legal proceeding is traumatic and stressful at best, and often a terrible experience taking a toll financially and emotionally. Suing someone or being sued is a highly charged, confrontational experience that can generate very bitter feelings and impose a severe strain. Dealing with lawyers, even one's own lawyer, in these settings can either make the situation better or worse depending on how effectively you can communicate with him or her.

Even talking to a lawyer about things involving nothing adversarial can be daunting - especially if the lawyer talks in terminology you don't understand or leaves out explanations and details you need. Talking about a will or power of attorney, for example, takes the ordinary non lawyer into a world of unfamiliar concepts and terms that are second nature to a competent lawyer.

Who is the "attorney in fact" and what does that mean? If the lawyer starts throwing out terms like trusts, heirs, executors, guardians, conservators, inheritance *per stirpes*, estate tax, inheritance tax, rule against perpetuities, and others the non-lawyer client can quickly feel confused, overwhelmed, frustrated or all of the above.

I've had clients say to me, "I know you explained this to me but I really don't understand it." When I hear that I kick myself for not doing a better job in the first place. I have witnessed lawyers talking down to their clients, which is atrocious. Many years ago I gained a good client with businesses and a large estate who came to me because his lawyer, in a good and prestigious law firm, presented him with

3

estate planning documents and said, "You just need to sign these, Albert. I could explain them but you wouldn't understand anyway." A couple of weeks later the man was in my office. After our meeting he told me he understood what I had told him and then related the story about his former lawyer by way to explaining why he had made the change.

I'm going to tell you something very important.

You have a right to understand what your lawyer is saying.

Your lawyer has a responsibility to talk to you in terms you can understand and to give you information you can use. Yes, some things are easier to explain than others. Some things are easier to understand than others. But unless you and your lawyer can communicate effectively with each other, which is a two-way street, you're not getting the professional service you deserve. The miscommunication could even result in your losing your legal due.

Likewise, your counsel has a legitimate expectation that you will communicate information fully and accurately so the lawyer can work for you effectively.

There are many reasons for the all too common experience of flawed communication between lawyer and client, and either the lawyer or the client or both may cause or contribute to the problem. The hope of this book is that it will help you to communicate effectively with your lawyer, feel more satisfied with your working relationship, and get better results from your experience with the legal profession and the legal system.

REMEMBER:

- *It's okay to be nervous. Not everyone talks to lawyers all the time.*
- *You are the client. Your lawyer works for you and should be trying to help you.*

- *You have a right to understand! Don't let legal jargon go unexplained. Ask for explanations.*
- *Good communication with your lawyer is key. If your lawyer confuses you or talks down to you, it's time to find a new lawyer.*
- *Almost any interaction with a lawyer can be stressful. Some legal matters are the most stressful things we experience.*
- *Be as clear as you can when you tell your lawyer what you want.*
- *Organize your thinking. You may want to write down names, dates, places, and other facts so you can keep them straight for your lawyer.*
- *Be respectful. Your lawyer's training and experience deserve your respect, but don't be afraid to ask questions.*

WHEN YOU SHOULD TALK TO A LAWYER

Legal problems are not do-it-yourself projects.

I realize that for many people lawyers are threatening or off putting. People often think of lawyers as arrogant or stuck up, and some certainly are or at least appear that way. And everyone worries about costs, as well they should.

But trying to handle your own legal problems can result in making things worse. Would you take out your own tonsils? Or pull your own tooth?

Years ago I had the occasion to settle an estate in which a young man died unexpectedly in his 30s. He ran a small chain of stores. His businesses were not incorporated and he had no clear arrangements to succession of the business or an orderly winding up of it should he die. He had notes about his estate plan he expected to be followed by family and associates, but to "save money" he had never made a will. You can easily imagine the unfortunate trials and difficulties his family faced settling his estate and winding up the business, at a considerable loss of value. Consulting a qualified lawyer could have avoided much or all of that and would have been well worth the cost.

Many people facing divorce or family struggles go it alone and even appear in court without an attorney. Among other reasons, people do this to save expense, keep things "simple," and avoid raising the level of confrontation any higher than it already has to be in such cases. This "pro se" representation in family law matters is so common that the court systems around the country have developed standard forms and helps to the unrepresented, including court appointed mediators and advisors. Depending on your state, you may find more or less help for the pro se litigant. The courts do their best to help and do a good job.

Yet I am afraid I have seen many instances of self-completed divorce forms and self-created agreements coming back to haunt people later, causing severe emotional and financial hardships for people who have already gone through a terribly trying personal and legal ordeal who have to reopen all the old wounds again later when their arrangements go wrong.

A few years ago I worked with a woman who had quite understandably pushed through her own divorce without a lawyer to save time and money, conceding on many points including assumption of debt, child and educational support, and medical bills. When her former husband failed to pay child support or fulfill other obligations, weaknesses and ambiguities in the agreement crippled her efforts to get justice.

Pleading inability to pay the husband nonetheless found the money to hire lawyers and fight her. He refused to pay educational costs or medical expenses for an 18-year-old child in college, in part because he had gotten into their self-created agreement a limit that contributions to higher education would only be made if they would not cause the party paying "financial harm," an ambiguous and meaningless term that thwarted any enforcement. I wouldn't say that having a lawyer in the first place would necessarily have made everything perfect, but a capable lawyer certainly could have negotiated more balanced terms and documented them clearly.

I could go on with these examples. You probably have heard similar stories or may even have experienced something similar. It simply isn't right to leave your family and friends at risk for lack of proper legal planning. It makes no sense to save some money now only to find yourself not legally protected in the future in your business, employment, investments, real estate, or contracts.

Lawyers Can Guide You to Other Professionals

Lawyers are connected to all sorts of other professionals that could be of help in your case or legal need. A good lawyer knows his or her own limits and recognizes when you need help from other professionals, such as surveyors, engineers, accountants, appraisers, financial advisors, insurance advisors, or medical or other technical experts. A lawyer with experience in the area of your needs will often have worked with the right professionals who will be effective working with you and can make reliable recommendations.

REMEMBER:

- *Just as you wouldn't try to take out your own tonsils, don't try to solve your own legal problems.*
- *If you put off getting legal advice, your situation could become worse.*
- *There's truth behind the legal adage, "Pay me now or pay me later."*
- *Don't be afraid. Find the right lawyer to work with and you can be comfortable.*
- *A lawyer can be a good resource to guide you to other professionals you need, such as an accountant or financial advisor.*

FINDING THE RIGHT LAWYER

Let's say you are ready to seek legal advice, how do you find the right lawyer? The best way is talking to people you know and trust who have worked with lawyers themselves on similar problems, either as clients or as professionals working in collaboration with the lawyer. In some cases, you may have a lawyer you worked with in the past who may not be qualified to handle what you need now but who can make a good referral for you.

For instance, the lawyer who handled your auto accident case a few years ago probably would not feel qualified to advise you on forming a business or the tax aspects of operating your business. But the accident lawyer likely would know lawyers who could, either by direct experience or reputation. Or vice versa; your lawyer who did your will could probably recommend a good lawyer for your divorce or auto accident case.

If you work with lawyers in a firm with other lawyers, the lawyers within the firm may have the necessary skills for most or all your legal needs in one place, bringing into the matters the people best qualified to help you. The internal referral will be made in good faith to serve your best interests, so usually you shouldn't feel slighted by it. But if you know it's important to you to have a particular lawyer working on your matter don't be afraid to insist on that lawyer, rather than being handed off to someone else, or maybe at least to have the lawyer you have confidence in stay involved in the matter for you to help in communication.

Lawyer referral services can be helpful also. The bar association in your state will often have lists of lawyers by areas of practice and locale.

It's good to know whether your lawyer is rated by Martindale Hubbell because only lawyers regarded by their peers as professionally reputable can be rated at all. Their ratings list lawyers as A, B, or C rated, again based on peer reviews. There are other rating services such as Best Lawyers in American, Chambers and Super Lawyers. There are good lawyers who don't rise to the top of these ratings for whatever reasons, but certainly having high ratings in these services is a good sign your potential lawyer is skillful and respected.

Another good indication that your possible lawyer is capable and well regarded is that he or she is included in honorary organizations within a legal specialty. For example, the American College of Trust and Estate Counsel (ACTEC) is an association of lawyers who are recognized experts in estate planning, wills, trusts, and probate proceedings. If you're looking for a lawyer to help you plan your estate or probate the estate of a deceased family member, it would be very reassuring to know that the lawyer you are planning to hire is an ACTEC member.

Ask your would-be lawyer if he has experience with your particular issue. Every lawyer has to start somewhere, and a younger or less experienced lawyer who works hard can still do a good job without the benefit of a lot of experience. On the other hand, experience builds judgment and knowledge that is practically impossible to replace even with diligent work and research.

If you do work with a relatively inexperienced lawyer who is in a firm with veteran lawyers, however, that can work well as you have assurance the lawyer has mentors to turn to for advice. And younger lawyers have passion and energy that sometimes the veteran may not match. So although I recommend a strong bias in favor of experience, you might prefer a newer lawyer in the right circumstances.

Above all, choose a lawyer who you like, who inspires your trust, and who communicates well with you. You could be spending a lot of time with the lawyer and depending on the nature of your legal business, this lawyer could be the man or woman shepherding you through one of your most difficult life experiences. Trust and confidence are vital. We all have our own personalities. The lawyer's personality should fit well with yours. You have to work well together. You have to like each other at the professional level at least, though not necessarily pals otherwise. Don't be afraid to take your time in finding a lawyer you feel comfortable with.

REMEMBER:

- *Word of mouth is a great way to find the right lawyer.*
- *Ask people you know and trust who they used for the kind of legal matter you have.*
- *Talk to others in your same business or line of work.*
- *Get recommendations from your accountant, financial advisor or other professionals.*
- *Check your potential lawyers' background with bar associations and ethics bodies.*

HOW YOU SHOULD TALK TO A LAWYER AND HOW THE LAWYER SHOULD TALK TO YOU

Plain English, please

Lawyers have a language all their own, so remember to ask for things in plain English.

In law schools law students go through three years of intense study and class discussion. Much of it is aimed at breaking down the self-assurance of law students and, after humbling them, teaching them to think a certain way and reason through problems. The basic method of legal reasoning is to gather all the facts of a problem and then look for general principles of the law that tell you what to do on those facts. This method of reasoning is tied to the history of the law in England and its development after coming to the Americas with the colonists.

The history of the law in England and America is the "common law," a development of legal principles by the decision of specific cases. When one man's cow wandered into his neighbor's lands, could he go get it back? If you made a pond on your land and it broke open and flooded your neighbor's field, were you liable in damages for that? What if you simply drained a swamp on your fields, causing the water to turn your neighbor's field into a marsh?

Or suppose you promised to buy a horse from a farmer who said the horse was young, strong and healthy, but not too long after you got it home it died, from an illness that was well under way when you bought it but unknown to you. Would the seller have to give your money back? Would it depend whether the seller knew the horse was ill? Maybe you promised to sell your farm to another, who gave you money to hold as a deposit until next month. When the buyer came back you had changed your mind and said you would refund the deposit. The buyer says you can't do that, you promised and I want this land. Must you sell?

As people brought these disputes to the courts and the judges decided them, their decisions, given orally on the spot, were taken down by scribes for the record. That way the interested persons knew what the decision was and others could refer to it.

Some of the oldest reports of these cases go back well into the middle ages. As the centuries passed courts looked back to these precedents to guide them in the cases they had to decide. If the facts of a current case were the same or similar to cases decided before, the courts could refer to that precedent to decide the same way.

This is why law students spend so much time reading court decisions and absorbing the method by which courts identify the important facts of a case and separate them from the unimportant facts. This is why your lawyer will need to get all the facts from you when you discuss a problem.

The other thing that happened when the law developed on a case by case basis was that legal principles were often identified and remembered by shorthand phrases that represented the legal rule. And given that many legal principles evolved long ago, at times when Latin was the language of scholarship, you often find them in Latin.

For example, some kinds of careless or negligent acts were so obviously bad the courts said, "The thing speaks for itself." Just because someone caused it to happen, that person was responsible. You set off a lighted firecracker in the town marketplace and it injures unsuspecting people around you. It's obvious that was dangerous and you should have known better. You're liable to the people you hurt. The thing speaks for itself. But of course the phrase could not be in English, it had to be Latin, or *res ipsa loquitur*. That means, "The thing speaks for itself."

So now you're a law student and you learn about this principle. You like it and you feel pretty smart, especially using that Latin. You start to hear other students talking about a case they read and saying things like, 'Oh yeah, that was a *res ipsa loquitur* case." Then a few days later they are even more sophisticated and say things like, "That's a simple *res ipsa* case."

Well the law and the legal system are full of these catch phrases, many in Latin that lawyers learn and then toss around amongst themselves and the courts. It's almost like studying for priesthood and learning the formula words. The law is not the only profession like this, of course. Art, medicine, engineering, and others all have their own key phrases or jargon. For all professionals it's a challenge to avoid hiding their meaning when talking to others who are not initiated into the vocabulary. And many of us like to show off our learning.

You have a meeting with your lawyer who says to you, "Well, Ms. Smith, I can see from what you're telling me you have as strong res ipsa case." Had you not just read my explanation of what that means, the lawyer's comments to you would not be very helpful, would they? But your lawyer is just thinking about what you told her and fitting your facts into the general legal principle that applies, just like it was hammered into her head in law school.

To become a lawyer, you have to learn the language. But when you communicate with a client you have to stop using that jargon and put the ideas back into language normal people use. Or at least if you must use the jargon terms first you have to explain them so that the client recognizes and understands them later, just like you do.

So, the point for you, the client, is to make sure your lawyer does not jargon you to death. If you don't understand a word or phrase say so, and get an explanation. If your lawyer can't or won't do that, you have the wrong lawyer.

Worse still, if your lawyer says something like, "That's just legalese we use, don't worry about it," or worst of all says, "You won't be able to understand that, just let me worry about it," then you really have the wrong lawyer.

If your lawyer uses confusing language or you can't understand him, the fault is the lawyer's, not yours. But if you don't insist on getting an explanation, then shame on you.

When you're talking to your lawyer to explain your problem, be ready to provide all the pertinent facts. Be thoroughly prepared and organize your thoughts.

We've talked about how important the facts are to every legal problem. Of course not all facts are necessarily relevant to the legal framework that will control your situation. What may seem important about your case to you may not necessarily be legally relevant. If your lawyer doesn't seem interested in some things that seem important to you, that may be why. But you can ask for an explanation.

Be specific. Give details. Tell your story chronologically. Begin at the beginning and try not to stray off into details or grievances that don't relate to the problem.

It's usually very important to tell your lawyer everything (the exception may be in criminal cases when telling your lawyer too much may prevent him from letting you testify later). Remember the very important rule that everything you tell a lawyer is confidential. Lawyers have a duty of loyalty to their clients, which includes a duty to preserve confidences and secrets of the client. Everything you tell your lawyer is confidential and cannot be disclosed without your permission. In litigation, lawyer-client communications are considered privileged, protecting you when you work with your lawyer.

Just as you want your lawyer to avoid legalese and professional jargon, you have to do the same. Explain the meaning of technical terms that have to be used in discussing your legal case or legal needs.

Most lawyers are very busy. You are entitled to the lawyer's time and attention and should insist on it. But at the same time you do not want to waste the lawyer's time (and your money) with a lot of talk off the topic.

GETTING YOUR QUESTIONS ANSWERED

Write down questions ahead of time. That way you won't forget to ask something and can be more relaxed when you talk to the lawyer. Talking to a lawyer can be intimidating, even if it's to your own lawyer. As you work with a lawyer and get to know her, especially if it is a business lawyer or lawyer representing you in ongoing matters other than a current dispute, this is easier. But even then, without writing down your questions you may forget something and spend frustrating time trying to get back in touch for an answer that would have been simple during your meeting.

Follow up and don't be afraid to ask questions. If you don't understand something, ask for it to be explained. It's ok to ask about confusing terms or what Latin phrases mean or where they come from. There are no stupid questions. If a lawyer makes you feel stupid for asking, you need another lawyer.

If your lawyer makes a recommendation make sure you ask to understand why. Ask for an explanation of the alternatives rather than just accept a single recommendation when you get the sense that there could be more than one possible approach. For one thing if you talk through the alternatives, you may know or realize something the lawyer has not, which in turn changes the lawyer's evaluation of the options. There may be facts that did not come out in earlier discussions that change things. I have many times had the experience of thinking I had a good solution to the client's problem only to see, as we discussed it further, that there may be another alternative I never even considered that's better, or at least needs to be in the mix. Sometimes I've misunderstood the client's wishes, and then as we talk the client can say to me, "Oh, that's not really what I want to do."

If your lawyer explains and things still aren't clear, tell him you don't understand and ask him to explain it in a different way. It may be helpful to use examples to explain, or parallels to similar cases. Sometimes a simplified list or chart is helpful, or writing in large letters on a white board or flip chart. If you are a visual learner, ask your lawyer to literally draw you a picture or a flow chart, as sometimes that actually is the best way to visualize and understand a complex document or transaction.

Most lawyers will welcome clients' questions and are happy to explain their recommendations (albeit sometimes in jargon or confusing language). Frankly I sometimes worry when a client is too accepting of my advice because it makes me wonder if the client really understands. I appreciate being trusted. It is an honor we enjoy often in the legal profession. But I like to be sure that the client understands what we will be doing and why, and is engaged in the decision making process.

Meeting expectations

Meeting expectations is a very important part of the working relationship between lawyer and client, and it goes both ways. The lawyer should be able to tell you exactly what they are going to do, how and when approximately – subject, of course, to the possibility that events beyond the lawyer's control (or yours) or the actions of courts or other parties will prevent or delay what is planned.

Likewise, the lawyer should be clear about what is expected of you and what the lawyer will need from you to accomplish important tasks. Make sure you have the lawyer's needs down accurately in your notes or ask for a follow up letter or memo from the lawyer to lay it all out.

When your lawyer asks for something, give it to her! When your lawyer asks you to do something (like keep a journal or making a record of events or communications), do it. And if she has a deadline that depends on you, be extra vigilant.

Though a lawyer has agreed to represent you, the lawyer is not bound to stick with you if you aren't helping the lawyer do her work or if you're not meeting your commitments to the lawyer. If this happens, a lawyer can withdraw even in a court case.

What about financial expectations? We know legal services are can be costly, sometimes very expensive. Nobody likes having to pay legal bills. It's important for you to meet your financial obligations to your lawyer. Lawyers are running a business and have to meet their expenses, too. And like other obligations, if you don't pay your lawyer according to the agreements between you for fees and payments, the lawyer can withdraw from representing you. It won't make it easier to find a new lawyer if your old lawyer stopped working because you didn't pay him.

Don't miss an appointment and if you are going to be late, call. Lawyers usually work under pretty tight schedules and can make good use of the time if you're not going to be able to keep an appointment. Lawyers don't typically charge for missed appointments, like other professionals and services, but of course that's not a reason to be inconsiderate about keeping scheduled appointments.

On the other hand, the lawyer should not keep you waiting. It's not like going to the doctor or the dentist, where waiting is common. If your lawyer regularly keeps you waiting or is late for scheduled appointments, you can and should complain about it. If you aren't satisfied, maybe you need a more punctual and considerate lawyer.

You never get a second chance to make a first impression so dress appropriately the first time you meet with a lawyer. I'm not telling you how you ought to present yourself or how you ought to look. But just make sure that the way you do choose to present yourself is the way that you want to be perceived. Likewise, the lawyer is making a first impression with you. If you don't like the way he or she presents to you maybe this is not the right lawyer.

When your lawyer asks you to do something, do it. Isn't this obvious? Yes, it is, but you would be surprised how often clients come the lawyer with urgent problems or needing immediate action and then they themselves dawdle or are even completely delinquent in following through with the things they're supposed to be doing. Your lawyer cannot be effective helping you if you are not faithful in fulfilling your agreed upon tasks or responsibilities.

- Understand it's not a bad thing if your lawyer says, "I don't know but I'll find out". Better to say he doesn't know than to pretend he does and give a wrong or misleading answer. If he doesn't know the answer to any of your questions, he may be incompetent.
- Part of talking to your lawyer is also listening, so listen carefully to what is being said and don't interrupt. Make notes of any questions.
- It's the lawyer's job to make sure that their clients understand as much as they want to about their issue and process.
- Ask when you will hear more, get updates and status reports on what to expect.

REMEMBER:

When you meet with your lawyer:

- *Write down your questions and bring them with you.*
- *If it would help, bring someone else with you.*
- *Bring anything the lawyer has asked you for.*
- *Be on time (lawyers usually don't keep you waiting).*
- *Don't be afraid to ask about fees and costs.*
- *Make sure you understand what your lawyer is telling you before you leave.*
- *Know exactly what (if anything) the lawyer expects you to do and when.*
- *Know what the lawyer is going to do next and when.*

GETTING RESULTS

Know what you want to achieve and be sure to tell your lawyer what you want to achieve as it may not be achievable. In your discussions you and your lawyer will talk about your legal problem and what you want to accomplish. Your lawyer in turn can tell you what the law permits or requires and how likely it is that what you would like to achieve can be accomplished through the law. It's important for you to listen to this and not to allow your own emotions or wishes to control your decisions without at least giving due consideration to your lawyer's advice.

If there's a choice between different courses of action, ask the lawyer for a recommendation. Consider the ramifications, consequences of actions and what might go wrong and ask the lawyer why he's making the recommendation he is making.

If a lawyer tells you you can't do what you want, you should ask if there's something else you can do to meet or come close to your objective.

It's also possible to get another opinion or advice from another attorney if the advice you get at first disappoints or seems wrong to you. This is not to "shop around" for a lawyer who will tell you what you want to hear, but just to be sure you are getting good advice and understand it and the reasons for it.

People do change lawyers sometimes. It may be a good idea if you're not happy with your lawyer, do not feel comfortable, or don't feel the lawyer is zealously representing your interests. Just be sure that you're doing it for good reasons and not to get a lawyer who will push for what you want, whether warranted and prudent or not.

REMEMBER:

- *Know your goals and what you want to accomplish.*
- *Get your lawyer's advice on whether these are attainable goals. If not, get the lawyer to tell you what you can accomplish.*
- *Be ready to adjust your expectations if you must.*
- *Expect creativity and a positive attitude from your lawyer (and if you don't get that, change lawyers). Don't settle for only negative responses.*
- *Be realistic. A good lawyer will help you to understand the reality of your situation, which is the kind of advice you want.*

SOME PRACTICAL ADVICE FOR AN EFFECTIVE WORKING RELATIONSHIP

Ask your lawyer approximately when things will be done

Things can end up taking longer than expected for many reasons. The initial estimate can be too optimistic. Government authorities or local officials may move more slowly than anticipated. The action (or inaction) of adversaries or others may change the timetable significantly. But it's still reasonable to ask for an estimate of the time things will take at the beginning. And it's reasonable for you to check periodically and ask for the explanation should the original timetable not hold true.

A good lawyer will be keeping you informed of anything significant, so you shouldn't have to ask for information about important developments. But if you're feeling in the dark, don't be afraid to ask. Remember, your lawyer has an ethical duty to keep you reasonably informed and you are paying the bills.

Ask your lawyer what she's going to do and when

This is related to the first point but more specific. It's good to get a step-by-step plan from your lawyer. It may be simple. It may be complicated. It's also something that will need to be revised if things change or the circumstances warrant. But it will help you to understand and it's important to know what you can count on your lawyer to do, and what you cannot count on your lawyer to do.

There may also be others (accountants, surveyors, medical experts, bankers, for example) who are part of the process and have to act to accomplish your goals. It's important to know that and to know upon whom you are relying for particular tasks, be it the lawyer or someone else.

Make sure you understand what else you need to do to help your lawyer achieve your goals

Your lawyer may need you to do certain things, or to get certain information. It's just as important for you to understand that as to understand what your lawyer is doing. Maybe more important, because you can control what you do. If the lawyer is counting on you for information or to do something, then obviously your legal matter will suffer if you don't uphold your end.

For example, an estate planning attorney may need information about your assets, what you own, whose name title stands in, account balances and portfolio values, life insurance policies, and more. Your estate plan won't get done until you get the information to her. Or a personal injury lawyer may need for you to follow up fatefully on medical appointments or treatments, or to keep a journal of your pain or limitations. If you fail, that will hurt your case. In fact, ethics rules allow a lawyer to stop representing you if you don't fulfill the reasonable agreements between you and your lawyer on such matters.

If there's a division of tasks between your lawyers and other advisors, make sure you know who's doing what and when they'll be done and know your personal deadlines

It is very common, of course, for a legal problem or legal planning process to involve you, your lawyer, and other professional advisors or expert consultants such as accountants, insurance professionals, appraisers, surveyors, engineers, bankers and trust officers, and others.

In this situation it's critical that you know what you are supposed to do and when, and that you follow through. But you also want to know what the others are doing and when you should expect their tasks to be accomplished. Things may change. The timetable may change due to various reasons or circumstances beyond anyone's control.

Unless the responsibilities and expectations are laid out clearly for everyone, however, they may not get accomplished. People may fail to act simply because they did not realize their responsibilities. Or they may fail to act without good reasons, in which case you need to know that and may have to consider making changes.

Ideally this will be written down. Good lawyers will often write a letter or memorandum to you to summarize the steps that are to be taken, by whom, and when so that everyone knows. That's good service from the lawyer to help you, and to be sure the project goes forward as it ought to do. If you don't get such a written summary from your attorney, you might want to consider preparing one yourself and circulating that to the advisors for their information and concurrence.

Find out if there's any time limit, deadline or statute of limitation

Claims or possible lawsuits are usually subject to a time limit and have to be presented or processed in the correct way within those time limits. Typically, a suit for medical malpractice, for instance, must be brought within a relatively short time after the alleged act of negligence, say two years. As we all know there are deadlines to file tax returns and there are deadlines and due dates for many other actions. Your lawyer should know what these are and should advise you should make note of the important dates and keep track of them as another check to be sure nothing gets missed. Your lawyer should calendar key dates, too, but it's a good idea for you to note them yourself and help make sure nothing is done too late.

REMEMBER:

- *Ask your lawyer what she is going to do and, approximately, when things will be done.*
- *Ask your lawyer what you need to do and by when you need to do it.*
- *If there's a division of tasks between your lawyers and other advisors, make sure you know who's doing what and when they'll be done.*
- *Know your personal deadlines.*
- *Find out if there's any time limit, deadline or statute of limitation.*

FEES: WHAT AM I BEING CHARGED FOR

Naturally one of the most important things to you about hiring and working with a lawyer is knowing what it will cost. People have the general notion that lawyers are hugely expensive. I guess it is all relative, as they say, because what one person considers very costly may seem reasonable to another. And the value of legal services is not always obvious.

As I write this the government is talking about setting the minimum hourly wage at $10.10. Lawyers and other professionals charge far more than that per hour for their time, and for that matter so do auto mechanics or plumbers. Even outside the large urban markets lawyers today often charge $300 per hour or more, and in some firms or specialty practices the hourly rate could be much higher.

Why is this? Is there any reason other than greed?

Determining what anyone's services are worth is a tricky business. A lawyer's hourly rate is also a function of their expenses to do business. This historically includes salaries and benefits of relatively large numbers of employees, occupancy costs, administrative overhead, printing and copying costs, costs for communication, and costs for libraries and legal research tools. Lawyers have also invested at least three years in school and typically spend time and money every year of their professional careers on continuing legal education and conferences.

Legal knowledge and skill are valuable. Are they as valuable as what lawyers charge for their time and advice? I don't know.

In every state and all federal jurisdictions, lawyers are under a duty to charge only a reasonable fee for their work. Charging an excessive fee is considered unethical conduct and is subject to discipline.

In court proceedings considering an award of attorney's fees the court can review the reasonableness of the fee and adjust it if need be. In all states there are ethics authorities that can consider a complaint about the reasonableness of a fee, and they typically offer mediation or arbitration procedures to settle fee disputes.

If you think your lawyer has charged a fee that is excessive, first take it up with your lawyer. Most lawyers are completely willing to discuss these issues and often make adjustments.

If you cannot agree on the fee after discussing the dispute, find the state fee arbitration agency through your local bar regulatory authorities. This process typically involves filing a written request for the disagreement to be resolved by arbitration. The arbitration will likely be informal so that you have a fair chance to lay out your side of the dispute without it being overly complicated and without your having to hire a lawyer to represent you in the hearing itself.

If you go through such a procedure, though, you should have a good reason or reasons why you believe the lawyer has charged you too much. You should gather and organize any papers you have that confirm the fee you and the lawyer agreed on or that show the work the lawyer did or failed to do. Be prepared to give good reasons not merely that you do not want to pay the fee or think it is "too much."

Courts and ethics authorities generally consider objective factors to evaluate the reasonableness of the lawyer's fees, such as the following:

1. The time and labor required, the novelty and difficulty of the questions involved, and the skill required to perform the legal service properly.
2. The likelihood that the acceptance of the particular employment will preclude other employment by the lawyer.
3. The fee customarily charged in the locality or by the circumstances.
4. The amount involved and the results obtained.
5. The time limitations imposed by the client or by the circumstances.
6. The nature and length of the professional relationship with the client.
7. The experience, reputation, and ability of the lawyer performing the services

8.   Whether the fee is fixed or contingent on results obtained, and the uncertainty of actual collection of the fee when due.

These factors come from ethics rules developed by the American Bar Association that have been adopted (or adapted) by courts and ethics enforcement authorities in most states. Though all the factors can be relevant in a given situation, usually the time necessary to complete the tasks is considered the "lodestar." The legal fee doesn't have to be based on the least possible amount of time needed for the task instead of the time the lawyer actually did spend, but if it seems that an excessive amount of time has been spent the fee may be subject to reduction.

Flat or Fixed Fees

Sometimes lawyers will charge a "flat" or fixed fee for a task. Sometimes the lawyer will ask for a "retainer," a term that most people understand as an advance against future earned fees. Above all be sure that the lawyer and you have a clear agreement on the fees, how they will be determined, and how any advance payment is to be held and applied.

Contingent or Percentage Fees

The other very common type of non-hourly fee is the "contingent fee." People usually hear about these when they read or see a report of a large verdict or settlement in a court case, typically a personal injury or product liability case. The report will mention a legal fee of, say, 25 to 45 percent of the amount recovered, which tends to sound pretty steep. What such reports miss is why these fees are used and why they appear so large in reference to what the injured party receives.

The simple explanation is a contingent fee allows someone who couldn't afford to pay the costs of a suit and legal fees to pursue a claim that appears to have merit despite not having the money to do so.

Instead of asking the client to pay ongoing fees on an hourly basis, and asking the client to pay the costs of the suit such as experts, doctors, court costs, and fees, the lawyer advances all the costs and shares the risk that the case will be a success. This way, for example, a person injured as a result of medical malpractice can afford to pursue her claims without having to pay thousands of dollars for medical experts and consultations and other costs and without getting regular bills to pay along the way from the lawyer.

The costs of carrying on such a suit can be enormous because such cases require expert testimony from doctors, and costs of obtaining records and other research. Such litigation requires an expensive "discovery" process, including getting and copying records and taking depositions of witnesses.

A deposition is a process in which lawyers get to ask potential witnesses questions under oath to establish the facts. These depositions establish each witness's memory of the facts and his or her "story" if the facts are in dispute. They are very important to the preparation for trial and often turn up information that results in a settlement of the case. But they cost money: getting witnesses and trial lawyers to the same place, the time of the lawyers during the deposition (which can take days), and the costs of court reporting and transcription.

Lawyers are all different and will estimate their time to prepare a case based on the way things work in their courts, but a good guess is 3-4 days of preparing for every anticipated day of the trial, even after the foundation has been laid through discovery. It's easy to see how in even relatively ordinary cases folks encounter the costs of mounting a lawsuit can be overwhelming. However, the contingent fee gives people access to the system of justice who could never afford to mount that effort otherwise.

That said, it's very important to consider a contingent fee arrangement carefully. Typically, the fee is based on percentage of actual amounts recovered, somewhere between 25 and 40 percent, with one third being the most common. This will be a percentage of the net amount recovered after paying any bills you owe to doctors or hospitals, after repayment of any benefit amounts you may have received during the pendency of the case, and after all the costs we just talked about.

So depending on those factors the amount you and your lawyer will share according to the contingent fee agreement will be likely less, and could be significantly less, than the gross amount paid to you by the other side. In each case you and your lawyer will have to consider this very carefully in considering any settlement, as there are often ways to structure the settlement of the case that are better for you than others.

For example

Make sure that you have a written agreement with the lawyer for the fees to be charged, contingent or otherwise, so that you and the lawyer both know and understand the arrangement. That should avoid any disagreement later or any surprise or disappointment to you.

It's okay to ask for an estimate of the fee, but remember it will be only an estimate. This is a question that makes me nervous as a lawyer, honestly, not because I don't understand how important this is to the client or because I want to dodge the issue. It can just be so hard sometimes to estimate accurately the time you spend as an attorney, which is never under your complete control.

If the others involved, such as parties or lawyers on the other side, take up a lot of time that will increase the cost to my client. If my client takes a lot of my time, or is a client who requires a lot of my time to get him or her to follow up on requests, that will increase the cost. In any case, estimating the ultimate amount of legal fees is not exact. As a client you shouldn't let yourself be too fixated on the estimate as to what your costs will actually be, or at least not as the maximum they will be.

This means you don't want to waste time and money by being unprepared, unorganized, or not having all the facts and information the lawyer needs (ask ahead for what is needed) when you work with or meet with your lawyer.

Know that most lawyers have others deal with the financial details so their time can be spent on legal work. Thus if you have questions about billing or any of the charges your lawyer has made you will often start by speaking to non-lawyer personnel in a billing or finance office. This isn't to say, however, that you should feel the slightest bit reluctant to talk to the lawyer himself or herself if you have lingering questions or concerns that the fees charged were not according to your agreement. Sometimes people just make mistakes and there can be overcharges you can correct easily by asking for an explanation.

Legal fees and the lawyer's bills

As we noted there are various fee arrangements that you might make with your lawyer. Whatever the arrangement, make sure that you get regular information about the lawyer's fees, how they're mounting up, and what you owe currently. Ask for regular bills (I recommend monthly) and if you don't understand the bill, ask questions. It's okay to ask the lawyer to explain charges.

If they seem too high, you may be misunderstanding or there could be a mistake. In busy law firms despite good intentions sometimes charges that belong to one client end up on the bill for another. Unless the bill is going to be contingent a flat fee, or some other non- hourly arrangement, ask the lawyer to give you itemized bills showing time spent, by whom, and the charge on each entry. This can avoid confusion.

- Ask for regular bills, monthly if possible
- Ask for the bills to be broken down by time, the attorney doing the work, and what it was
- Review your bills when you get them
- Ask questions if you need to
- Pay your bills as agreed between you and the lawyer.

- *Ask for regular bills, monthly if possible.*
- *Ask for the bills to be broken down by time, the attorney doing the work, and what it was done.*
- *Review your bills when you get them.*
- *Ask questions if you need to.*
- *Pay your bills as agreed between you and the lawyer.*

The good lawyer is not the man who has an eye to every side and angle of contingency, and qualifies all his qualifications, but who throws himself on your part so heartily, that he can get you out of a scrape.

Ralph Waldo Emerson

The leading rule for the lawyer, as for the man of every other calling, is diligence. Leave nothing for to-morrow which can be done to-day.

Abraham Lincoln

Glossary of Legal Terms[1]

This is a list of terms that come up often in legal matters and the legal system that can be confusing to people who do not work in the law regularly. The definitions are not a complete statement of the legal principles but only a simple statement hoped to be clear and helpful to you.

A

Acknowledge - To swear or affirm to a notary public or other officer that you have signed or agreed to a document. This "acknowledgement" is usually required for a deed, contract, lease or other document to be recorded in a public record office as it verifies the validity of the document.

Acquittal, acquitted - A jury verdict that a criminal defendant is not guilty, or the finding of a judge that the evidence is not enough to support a conviction. Some believe this should be changed to "not proven guilty." The person whose case ends in acquittal is said to have been "acquitted."

Admissible - When trying to prove a case, parties offer evidence in the form of testimony of witnesses, documents, and other forms of proof. There are rules in court about what evidence may be presented. If the evidence is "admissible" under those rules, the evidence can be considered by a jury or judge in civil and criminal cases.

Adversary proceeding - We say our legal system is an "adversary" system. This means that we have decided the best way to get at the truth and a just result is to have the contending parties present their best cases to a neutral decision maker, such as a judge or jury. An "adversary proceeding," then, is a lawsuit, administrative agency case,

---

1 A number of these definitions have been adapted from the guide to legal terminology posted by the US Government on its web site for the federal judiciary, www.uscourts.gov/Common/Glossary.aspx, which I believe to be in the public domain.

arbitration or similar process in which two or more parties represented by lawyers try to convince the decision maker to decide in their favor. This is the heart of the American legal system, based on the idea that the best way to get to the truth and to get a fair result is for parties to have their own advocates. In some other places, such as many European courts, the court system itself takes a more active role in the investigation of the matter, and the parties' advocacy role is more limited.

Affidavit - A written or printed statement made under oath. Giving an affidavit is a serious matter. You are swearing to the truth of the statements in the affidavit just as you would when testifying under oath in a court.

Alternative dispute resolution (ADR) - This has been a growing trend, both to relieve overcrowded court dockets and to seek speedier and less costly ways to resolve legal disputes outside the courtroom. ADR may be non-binding, such as the use of a mediator to try to help the parties reach their own settlement. It may be biding such as referral to an arbitrator who hears the case and makes a legally binding decision.

Appeal - A request made after a trial by a party that has lost on one or more issues that a higher court review the decision to determine if it was correct. To make such a request is "to appeal" or "to take an appeal." One who appeals is called the "appellant." The other party is the "appellee."

Assets - The legal term "asset" is used to describe something a person owns. It can be property of all kinds, including real estate and personal property. Personal property can be "tangible," like furniture, jewelry, and other physical objects, or "intangible," like stocks and bonds, bank accounts, and other valuable rights.

Assume - The legal term "assume," as in assume a debt or contract, means to agree to continue performing duties under the contract or lease that creates the duties. This usually means stepping into another's shoes to take over the obligations.

B

Bankruptcy - This is the technical term for the process a person or business can go through to be relieved of debts that the bankrupt cannot pay. The bankruptcy courts are all federal courts and they apply a federal law that is the same nationwide. Under the supervision of the federal bankruptcy court the debts may be modified or eliminated to enable the debtor to get a fresh start financially. Creditors can participate to protect their interests.

Bankruptcy trustee - This is the person appointed by the bankruptcy court to supervise the bankruptcy proceeding, and to represent the interests of the bankruptcy estate and the debtor's creditors. The person or business going through the bankruptcy can have an attorney to represent his, her or its interests, as the trustee does not.

Burden of proof - This is a term that relates to how someone proves a case in court. When the case is presented, one party has the burden of proof to present evidence that shows that party's claim is valid. In civil cases, a plaintiff generally has the burden of proving his or her case. In criminal cases, the government has the burden of proving the defendant is guilty. Because the person who has to prove the case will lose if he or she fails to meet that burden, it is very important who bears this burden. A person with a good claim may not be able to win a case because of the inability to get all the evidence needed to prove it.

C

Case law - The law established by court decisions, also called "legal precedent." This is the foundation of "common law," based on tradition and judicial decisions.

Cause of action - A legal claim. When the law recognizes a right to be enforced by the legal system, a legal action may be commenced to enforce that right. The individual claims in that legal action are called "causes of action."

Chapter 11 - A bankruptcy in which a business is not liquidated but allowed to continue in business. The business can be a corporation, other entity, or individual. A Chapter 11 debtor proposes a plan of reorganization to keep its business alive and pay creditors over time.

Chapter 13 - The chapter of the Bankruptcy Code providing for the adjustment of debts of an individual with regular income, often referred to as a "wage-earner" plan. Chapter 13 allows a debtor to keep property and use his or her disposable income to pay debts over time, usually three to five years.

Class action - A lawsuit in which one or more members of a large group, or class, of individuals or entities sue on behalf of the entire class. The court must find that the claims of the class members contain questions of law or fact in common before the lawsuit can proceed as a class action.

Clerk of court - The court officer who oversees administrative functions, especially managing the flow of cases through the court.

Collateral - Property that is promised as security for the payment of a debt. The security is usually confirmed by a written agreement that describes the rights and duties of the parties. Sometimes collateral can be secured by physically delivering to the creditor, such as when a stock certificate or a bond is given to the creditor to hold.

Common law - The legal system that originated in Medieval England and is now in use in the United States. This law is "common" in the sense that it relies on the development of commonly applied legal principles in a historical succession of court decisions. As courts reason their way through specific cases, they develop principles that they can apply in similar future cases. This was why law publishers began to print books containing the decisions of the courts so lawyers and other courts could read them for guidance in deciding future cases. Courts and lawyers call these former cases "precedent" and expect them to be relied on for certainty in future matters. Courts apply the concept of "*stare decisis,*" another Latin phrase meaning "to stand by things decided," when relying on former precedent to decide new cases. Although courts usually follow past deci-sions, sometimes they "overrule" them when changes in conditions warrant. Because the courts decide specific cases and do not have the power to make general laws by leg-islating, common law principles can be changed by legislation. In fact, sometimes state legislatures or the Congress pass laws directly aimed at changing the legal rules a court has defined. This is called legislatively overruling prior precedent.

Complaint - A written statement that begins a lawsuit. In the complaint the plaintiff (the one who brings the suit) details the claims against the defendant or defendants (the one or ones being sued). Court rules often say the complaint should be a short, plain statement of the claims for relief. Generally, there are no "magic words" required in court pleadings today as long as they give the other side fair notice of the claims. This does not stop attorneys from sometimes submitting very lengthy and detailed complaints and other pleadings to lay out their case fully.

Consumer bankruptcy - A bankruptcy case filed to reduce or eliminate debts that are primarily consumer debts.

Consumer debts - Debts for personal, as opposed to business, needs.

Contingent fee - A fee charged by a lawyer that is paid only upon a successful out-come of the case. Such a fee arrangement enables the person with a claim to pursue it without all the upfront expenses of hiring a lawyer and developing the case. It gives people who might have valid claims but not the means to pursue them access to the justice system. In all states the courts regulate the amount of such fees and how they can be earned, and typically require a written agreement. The fee is a percentage of the damages recovered, usually 25-45 percent though the amounts vary. The plaintiff in the contingent fee case must also bear the costs of the case, such as the fees of doc-tors or other expert witnesses, which are deducted from what is paid to the plaintiff at the end of the case.

Contract - An agreement between two or more people or businesses to do or not to do a particular thing. If it meets the requirements of the law, a contract will be enforced by the courts if a party does not carry it out. Litigation for breach of contract is one of the most common cases brought into our courts. To be enforced as a contract, the agreement must be clear enough to show what the parties have agreed to do, the agreement must be to do things that are legally permitted, and the contract must be supported by "consideration." Consideration means something of value, which could be money, goods, services, or actions. In some cases a contract has to meet additional requirements to be enforced. For example, although oral contracts are usually enforceable contracts to buy and sell land typically have to be in writing or they cannot be enforced.

Conviction - A court judgment of guilt against a criminal defendant.

Counsel - This noun can refer to legal advice or to the lawyer in a legal matter or case. Lawyers give their advice and counsel to their clients. The lawyer is called, "counsel," as in when a judge says, "Counsel may proceed with her next witness."

Court - Government entity authorized to resolve legal disputes. Judges sometimes use "court" to refer to themselves in the third person, as in, "The court has read the briefs."

Court reporter - A person who makes a word-for-word record of what is said in court, generally by using a stenographic machine, shorthand or audio recording, and then produces a transcript of the proceedings upon request. In earlier times court reporters or stenographers had to write out the words of the judges, witnesses and lawyers while they were talking, usually in shorthand. This was still common as recently as the 1970's in America, before mechanical shorthand machines or electronic recordings became prevalent as they are today.

D

Damages - Money that a defendant pays a plaintiff in a civil case if the plaintiff has won. Damages may be compensatory (for loss or injury) or punitive (to serve as an example and deter future misconduct).

Debtor - A person who owes money and has filed a petition for relief under the Bankruptcy Code.

Defendant - In a lawsuit the person who brings the case (plaintiff) brings it against one or more people or other entities, called the defendant. The defendant is defending against the claims in the lawsuit. In a criminal case, the defendant is the person accused by the government of committing the crime.

Debtor's plan - In bankruptcy cases, this is a debtor's detailed description of how and when the debtor proposes to pay creditors' claims. For a court to accept the plan it will have to show how the debts will be paid fully or in part over a fixed time period.

Declaratory judgment - A court decision that gives a judge's statement about someone's legal rights. A declaratory judgment spells out legal rights rather than awarding damages as such.

Deed - A writing that transfers the ownership of real estate from one owner or owners to another owner or owners. Typically to be effective the deed must identify the person(s) transferring the property (Grantor) and the person(s) receiving the property (Grantee). It must identify or describe the property. Sometimes the "description" is simply a reference to an earlier deed and will say the current deed conveys "all and the same" property. Sometimes the description is what is called a "metes and bounds" description. This means that in words the deed actually describes the beginning point and boundaries of a shape that is the parcel of land on the ground. A surveyor can develop a very exact metes and bounds description by going out onto the land and setting the courses with a compass and measuring the distances exactly. Many disagreements arise over property boundaries and descriptions and every year people bring many lawsuits over such disputes. It is very important to be sure that if you are buying or selling real estate, the description is clear and accurate.

De facto - Latin, meaning "in fact" or "actually." Something that exists in fact but not as a matter of law. This phrase can be used to describe a situation in which people are living or acting as though they have a legal arrangement, but they don't.

Default judgment - A judgment that gives the plaintiff the relief sought in the complaint because the defendant has failed to appear in court or otherwise respond to the complaint.

De jure - Latin, meaning "in law." This can be the opposite of "de facto," meaning that the actions or arrangements of people are indeed authorized and made valid by law.

De novo - Latin, meaning "anew." It is used to described as situation in which a hearing or proceeding is done over, started over. A trial de novo, for example, is a completely new trial of a matter that has already been fully presented to a court before. Sometimes a de novo proceeding is granted because the earlier proceeding was defective in some way. Sometimes it is just provided for to give people a fresh and unbiased chance to present their case to a different or higher authority. In a de novo proceeding nothing that happened before is binding on the new decision maker.

Deposition - This is part of the process known as "discovery" in which parties to a legal proceeding have an orderly way to get information. The deposition is sworn oral testimony given before a court reporter. Parties take depositions of other parties, or potential witnesses to get information and to get the person being deposed committed under oath so he or she cannot say something different later in trial. Sometimes the deposition is taken to preserve the testimony of a person who may not be available later.

Discharge - A bankruptcy term to describe the release through the bankruptcy of a debtor from personal liability for debts. Some debts are not dischargeable in bankruptcy, such as many forms of fines or penalties, taxes and student loans. After the discharge, creditors owed discharged debts cannot take any action against the debtor or the debtor's property to collect them. The discharge also prohibits creditors from communicating with the debtor regarding the debt, including through telephone calls, letters, and personal contact.

Disclaimer - A disclaimer is aimed at telling you what you cannot count on. For example, in a contract to buy goods you will often see a disclaimer of warranties, meaning the usual things you might expect the manufacturer to stand behind will be eliminated or limited by the written terms of your purchase. If you're presented a written contract, bill of sale, or other legal document with a disclaimer in it you should read that very carefully and if need be ask questions to be sure you understand what rights or benefits are being taken away from you.

Discovery - Procedures used to obtain disclosure of evidence before trial. This process seeks to avoid "trial by ambush" by allowing parties through their lawyers to collect evidence under court supervision. The "discovery" process can include (a) asking for sworn answers to written questions (interrogatories), (b) asking for access to records or documents (requests for production), (c) asking to be allowed to inspect or test physical objects, and (d) making a witness or party give a disposition, in which the person answers questions under oath before a court reporter. In today's litigation the lawyers usually want to put a lot of time and effort into discovery and preparation so that when the case is actually tried they have all the relevant facts and have a good idea what all witness will say when they testify. The discovery process takes time and can be costly but it is the key to being successful in most instances. Another valuable practical function of discovery is that once all parties know what the facts are, and what evidence they will be able to present in court, they have a much better idea of the likely outcome of their case. This in turn helps them decide whether to settle the case without the risks and costs of trial and what settlement would be reasonable.

Docket - A log containing the complete history of each case in the form of brief chronological entries summarizing the court proceedings.

Due process - In the United States Constitution and state constitutions we find a fundamental notion that citizens should not lose their lives, their liberty, or their property without "due process of law." In criminal law, the constitution guarantees that a defendant will receive a fair and impartial trial before being punished by the government. In civil law, due process rights protect someone facing an adverse action under government authority threatening liberty or property. For instance, before a government agency can take away a person's license to engage in an occupation, it must give the person notice of the possible adverse action and an opportunity to be heard before the government takes the action.

Durable power of attorney - People can give others the authority to act for them in their legal and financial affairs. This makes the person they authorize their "agent." The writing used to grant this authority is called a power of attorney. The law treats this as a grant by consent, meaning the person who gives the authority can revoke it. If the person who gives the authority becomes mentally disabled, he or she is no longer able to consent to anything. For this reason, traditionally the law considered a power of attorney to be revoked automatically when a person became mentally incompetent. But that is the very time when the power of attorney is most often needed, so now laws around the country allow a person to say in a power of attorney that it is not revoked by disability. That is why such a power of attorney is called "durable," because it carries on despite a disability affecting the power to consent. It is important to be sure that if you give a power of attorney it has this feature unless you don't want it for some reason.

E

Easement - This is a real estate term and it refers to a right for one party to make use of the land owned by another party. A classic example is if you needed to cross your neighbor's land to get to a farm field at the back of your land, your neighbor might grant you an easement to travel over the neighbor's land. Ideally the easement would be in a written deed or other document that can be recorded in a public records office giving notice of your rights. The easement can describe the location and any limitations or restrictions. Writing the legal documents to create and describe easements requires care and skill and should not be left to informal arrangements that can create problems or uncertainty in the future. Like insufficient real estate descriptions, poorly drafted easements are the source of a great deal of real estate litigation.

Equitable, equity - Pertaining to civil suits in "equity" rather than in "law." In English legal history, the courts of "law" could order the payment of damages and could afford no other remedy (see damages). A separate court of "equity" could order someone to do something or to cease to do something (*e.g.*, injunctions or orders of specific performance to sell property). In American jurisprudence, the federal courts have both legal and equitable power, but the distinction is still an important one. A trial by jury is normally available in "law" cases but not in "equity" cases.

Evidence - Information procedural rules permit to be presented in testimony or in documents to persuade the fact finder (a judge or jury, or an arbitrator) to decide a case in favor of one side or the other. In court proceedings rules of evidence regulate what information the parties can present. The kind of information we rely on all the time about what another person said or did not say might be called "hearsay" and not be allowed in a court case because the person who made the statement is not there to testify. Rules of evidence are aimed at assuring the truth and integrity of the information on which the decision is based. The rules sometimes also prevent evidence most of us would consider reliable from being heard.

Exemptions, exempt property - To protect people from having all that they own taken by creditors, the Bankruptcy Code or applicable state laws permit a debtor to keep certain assets or dollar value from their unsecured creditors. For example, in some states the debtor may be able to exempt all or a portion of the equity in the debtor's primary residence (homestead exemption), or some or all "tools of the trade" used by the debtor to make a living (*i.e.*, auto tools for an auto mechanic or dental tools for a dentist). The availability and amount of property the debtor may exempt depends on the state the debtor lives in.

Ex parte - A proceeding brought before a court or other tribunal by one party only, without notice to or challenge by the other side. Because our concepts of justice and fairness require that both sides to a dispute be heard before any decision, the law limits the circumstances in which parties can proceed *ex parte*. A good example is actions to put a lien or attachment on property in an emergency, when the property might be damages or removed by the other party (*e.g.*, a bank account) if the other party were to be notified in advance. Even when the law allows an action to be taken *ex parte*, it usually limits the scope or time of that action until notice can be given and the other party has a chance to be heard. Thus the relief granted *ex parte* is typically only temporary.

Ex post facto - Another Latin phrase meaning something taking place after the act being judged. For example, an *ex post facto* law is a law that makes something illegal or criminal after people have done it. This is clearly not just as a person cannot govern his or her conduct by a legal standard that does not yet exist, and therefore should not face consequence for failing to obey that standard. The Constitution prohibits such laws.

F

Felony - A serious crime. Historically it was used to describe crimes that could result in forfeiture of property or death. Lesser crimes are called misdemeanors. The distinctions between the types of crimes and punishments for them are today spelled out in laws and statutes enacted by the federal government or the states. In modern practice, this dividing line is that a felony is usually punishable by at least one year in prison. Conviction of a felony may also carry with it more significant long term consequences, such as legal disabilities that remain with the convicted felon for life (*e.g.,* a prohibition on owning firearms).

File - When speaking of legal matters, to "file" something typically means to place a paper in the official custody of the clerk of a court to enter into the files or records of a case or in the official custody of a government official who maintains public records. Whether a paper has been properly filed and filed on time is often a crucial question to determine valuable property rights or legal protections. If you are dealing with a legal matter in which your rights depend on filing something, you should make sure it is filed and filed on time.

Fraudulent transfer - Someone who owes money or who knows another person has a claim against him or her might try to protect assets from that debt or claim by hiding them away through a transfer to someone else for less than full value. The law sees such attempted transfers aimed at defeating legitimate debts or claims made with intent to defraud or for which the debtor receives less than the transferred property's value fraudulent, and therefore void. The law provides a right to recover the fraudulently transferred assets if possible and sometimes adds penalties such as damages of multiple times the value transferred, interest, and legal fees and costs.

G

Garnish - One thing a creditor can do to try to collect money is to ask the debtor's employer to make wage payments to the creditor instead. The legal term for this is to garnish. Laws limit the availability of this remedy so that the debtor can still receive enough of the wages to live.

Guardian - People who do not have the legal capacity to make their own financial or legal decisions may need protection. The law has long provided systems under court supervision for persons who need that protection to have someone appointed to watch over them, and that person is traditionally called a guardian. The guardian usually has the ability to make decisions for the protected person about living arrangements, personal care and health, and such matters as education. A guardian may or may not have control of the person's finances as well, or the financial protections may come from a person appointed just for that purpose (often called a conservator) or trustee. One strong reason to grant someone power of attorney is it avoids the possible need for a future legal guardianship with the expense and intrusion that involves (See durable power of attorney).

Guardian *ad litem* - This is a guardian appointed by the court for a specific case, typically to represent the interests of minor children or mentally incompetent adults who could be affected by the proceedings.

Grand jury - As a safeguard against ill-founded or abusive criminal prosecutions, our legal system provides for charges to be screened by a preliminary review by a body of citizens who listen to evidence of criminal allegations presented by prosecutors to determine whether there is probable cause to believe an individual committed an offense. As the name implies, the grand jury is larger than the typical trial jury, usually something between 12 and 24 grand jurors. It is not a full trial of the case but rather a mostly one sided presentation of the evidence the government believes warrants the prosecution. If the grand jury agrees it will issue an authorization for the prosecution stating the charges to be brought, which is usually called an indictment.

H

Habeas corpus - Latin, meaning "you have the body." A writ of *habeas corpus* generally is a judicial order forcing law enforcement authorities to produce a prisoner they are holding, and to justify the prisoner's continued confinement. The historical purpose of this was to prevent a person from being locked up indefinitely without any information for family or friends to find out where the person was being held. In recent years' state prisoners have used this process to try to get federal judges to review state prosecutions they claim violated their federally protected rights.

Hearsay - Evidence from a witness who does not personally know the facts but instead will testify about what someone else said was the fact, which is offered to prove the fact is true. Because the judgment of truth is being made based on what someone said who is not testifying, and subject to questioning, the hearsay evidence is usually considered less reliable than direct evidence. The witness did not personally see or hear the matter in question and has no direct knowledge of it, but heard about it from someone else. For example, the question might be to the witness to say what someone else said happened in a car accident. The hearsay evidence could also be in the form of a document or report about something offered to prove the truth of its contents. For example, everything we read in a newspaper is hearsay. With some exceptions, hearsay generally is not admissible as evidence in a court trial. In some other proceedings, however, hearsay that seems reliable may be accepted. There are also exceptions to the rule, such as for official reports and records, or for some hearsay statements that are inherently reliable, like what a person blurts out in excitement or an admission of a fact harmful to the person who made the hearsay statement. In our day to day lives we rely on hearsay all the time, when we read the paper or listen to the news, or when we ask our family, friends, or associates what someone else said. But in legal proceedings the stakes are higher.

I

Impeachment - In evidence rules, this is the term for calling a witness's testimony into doubt. This is usually done by showing that the testimony the witness is now giving is not accurate in some respects or contradicts what the witness said under oath before. For example, if the witness testified in a deposition that the traffic light was yellow, but at trial says it was green, the previous sworn deposition testimony can be used to cast doubt on the witness's testimony in court.

In camera - Latin, meaning in chambers. This refers to a review of evidence or some aspect of a case in the closed chambers of the judge outside the presence of a jury and the public. This might be done to take evidence from a child or vulnerable witness. It might be done to review evidence that is confidential or might be unfair or prejudicial to someone in the case.

Indictment - The formal charge issued by a grand jury stating that there is enough evidence that the defendant committed the crime to justify having a trial. See also information.

Information - A formal accusation by a government attorney that the defendant committed a misdemeanor or other crime that the government can prosecute without first getting a grand jury indictment. See also indictment.

Injunction - A court order that directs one or more persons to take or not to take some action. Injunctions are usually very specific and limited because they restrict people from doing what they otherwise would have a legal right to do, and if the person violates the injunction there can be serious consequences. That makes it very important what the injunction says. A court will sometimes issue a temporary or "preliminary" injunction to maintain the status quo until the court conducts more complete proceedings to determine whether to make the injunction permanent.

Interrogatories - A form of discovery consisting of written questions to be answered in writing and under oath.

J

Joint custody - An arrangement in a family law proceeding for parents of children to share custody and care of the children following a divorce. Such arrangements need to be specific and clear and should be put into an order from the court that can be legally enforced in the future to avoid strife.

Joint venture - A business combination between two or more firms to carry out a business or specific project. Usually a joint venture is limited to one business opportunity, such as development of a product or property, avoiding any general or continuing partnership. The businesses involved may form a new entity to carry out the joint venture or may simply agree on how they will cooperate to carry out their project. It is best to have a clear agreement in writing to specify (among other terms) what the venture will be, the contributions, roles and responsibilities of each party, how costs and profits will be shared, and when and how the joint venture will terminate.

Judge - An official of the judicial branch of the federal or a state government with authority to decide lawsuits brought before courts. People with judicial power and responsibility are also sometimes called justices or magistrates. The law creating a court may limit the authority of its judges to certain types of cases (*e.g.,* the United States Tax Court, which hears only federal tax disputes), cases involving disputes of more or less than a stated amount in controversy, or certain types of remedies.

Judgment - The official decision of a court finally deciding the dispute between the parties to the lawsuit.

Jurisdiction - The legal authority of a court to hear and decide a certain type of case. It also is used as a synonym for the geographic area over which the court has territorial jurisdiction to decide cases.

Jurisprudence - The study of law and the structure of the legal system.

Jury - The group of persons selected to hear the evidence in a trial and render a verdict on matters of fact. Historically a jury was twelve persons, but now juries are sometimes some number between six and twelve. See also grand jury.

Jury instructions - In a court case tired before a jury, the final step before the jury begins to decide the case is for the court to instruct the jury about its responsibilities and to explain the law that applies to the case. The jury has the duty to weigh all the evidence that it has and decide what the facts are, but it must take the law as it exists and apply it according to the judge's explanation. So in the instructions or charge to the jury, the judge gives directions to the jury before it begins deliberations regarding the factual questions it must answer and the legal rules that it must apply. Because this is so important, the parties to the case are allowed to submit requests to the judge in advance for how to describe the legal principles the jury is to apply. In some cases, there is room for argument about the legal principles that should control the decision or what words to use in explaining them. Because legal rules can be very complicated, judges try to explain them clearly and simply for jurors as best they can without being inaccurate.

K

L

Lawsuit - A legal action filed in a court. The person who starts the lawsuit is called the plaintiff. The person against whom the plaintiff brings the lawsuit is the defendant. The typical lawsuit is based on a complaint that the defendant failed to perform a legal duty which resulted in harm to the plaintiff. Some lawsuits seek a declaration of the legal rights and duties of the parties, such as who is the lawful owner of property, so they know their rights. Some lawsuits are brought to challenge the validity of laws or regulations issued by the government.

Lease - Under a lease the owner or real estate of personal property grants someone else the right to use the property. The historical origins of this arrangement involved lands that the owner leased to another to farm, so the owner was called the "landlord" and the person authorized the "tenant." When the property to be leased is personal property, such as a machine or vehicle, the term "lessor" is often used for the owner and "lessee" for the person leasing the property. But the terms can be used in either kind of lease. Under general principles of law, the person leasing the property has all the rights to it of an owner even to the exclusion of the real owner. That is, unless otherwise agreed, if a landlord rents real property to a tenant the tenant has all the rights to the property and can keep the landlord off it. Usually, however, the parties enter a written lease of the property to define the rights of the tenant/lessee, and reserved rights of the landlord/lessor, the rent to be paid for the use of the property, how long the lease will last and whether it can be renewed or extended, who has to maintain and insure the property, and more. Residential property leases can be detailed, but commercial leases usually much more so. A commercial lease is a very complex document in most instances and all the terms a critical to how well the arrangement will work for both parties.

License - A license is a right to use property just as a lease is, but it is generally considered conferring much more limited rights and unless otherwise agreed is normally considered revocable. That means the owner of the property can allow someone else to use and take back that permission at any time unless there is an agreement otherwise. A license can be granted to use real estate or undeveloped land for specific or limited purposes, such as to mine minerals. The term appears most often for intellectual property, like copyrights, patents, or trademarks. The owner of an invention or technology, for example, may grant another person or firm the right to use that know how in another business in exchange for the payment of agreed upon amounts or amounts based on the income the holder of the license gets from using the licensed property. Although there are many styles of writing license agreements, the terminology in a license is usually "licensor" for the person who gives it, "licensee" for the person who gets it, and "royalty" for the payments made to the licensor by the licensee.

Lien - A claim or charge on specific property to secure payment of a debt or performance of an obligation. The lien means that if the owner of the property does not pay or perform, the one holding the lien will have the right to take the property or sell it. Lien is a broad term that can apply to any charge against property. Another term for it is encumbrance. As to real estate the term "mortgage" is typically used to describe a lien granted against the real property by the owner. Laws sometimes create liens to protect people who provide goods or services, such as contractors, builders or suppliers who often enjoy the protection of liens created by statute that they can enforce if they are not paid for a project or materials. Some laws create liens in favor of the government, such as liens to secure payment of taxes.

Litigation - A broad term for a case, controversy, or lawsuit. Participants (plaintiffs and defendants) in lawsuits are called litigants.

Liquidation - The sale of property with the proceeds to be used for the benefit of a claimant or creditors. It can also refer to the process of dissolving a corporation or other business entity so that its assets can be distributed to the shareholders or other owners.

Liquidated damages - Sometimes it is difficult to measure or prove exactly the dollar damages someone will suffer from a breach of contract. For example, if a breach of a commercial contract presents the innocent party form carrying on its business effectively, we know the innocent party is harmed but it may be hard to measure the extent of that harm. Parties to a contract may agree that because exact measurement of loss is difficult or impossible they will set a formula or fixed amount of damages for a breach of contract. As long as their agreement reflects a reasonable estimation the courts will enforce it, but the courts generally will not enforce a clause that is arbitrary and amounts to a fine or penalty for breach of contract.

Loan - Generally a loan is the giving of money to a person or firm upon the promise to pay it back on agreed upon terms. There are many types of loans and the arrangements for them can be quite complicated. But the essential terms are how much the lender will lend, how and when the borrower will pay it back, whether interest will be charged and if so at what rate, and whether the loan will be secured by property of the borrower that the lender can sell to be paid (called collateral).

Loan agreement - A written agreement that describes the agreement of the lender to make the loan, the agreement of the borrower to accept the loan and pay it back, the terms of repayment and any security, and other terms the parties need to avoid any future uncertainties or difficulties carrying out the loan.

M

Misdemeanor - A criminal offense regarded as less serious than a felony, usually punishable by one year of imprisonment or less. See also felony.

Mistrial - A trial that is invalid because of some error in the way it was being conducted or some other flaw that makes it inherently unreliable, for example discovery that a juror had improperly investigated the facts outside the trial proceedings. The presiding judge has control over the conduct of a case and among other things must assure that the proceedings are regular and not tainted by any unfair errors or flaws. If the court learns of circumstances calling the validity of the trial into question, the court can and should investigate the matter and can declare mistrial if warranted. If the court declares a mistrial, the trial must start again with a different judge and if it has been a jury trial, the selection of a new jury.

Moot - Not subject to a court ruling because the controversy has not actually arisen, or has ended.

Motion - A written request by a litigant to a judge for an action or decision on an issue relating to the case. A motion may address a procedural issue, such as requesting more time to carry out certain functions or a delay in the schedule leading to a trial. It may request the court's help to get discovery. It may address a key issue affecting the outcome of the case or, in what is called a motion for "summary judgment," may actually dispose of the entire case when the court can rule on the legal issues without a formal trial.

Motion in Limine - This motion is made before trial requesting the court to prohibit the other side from presenting, or even referring to, certain evidence on the grounds that it is not proper under the rules of evidence or could be so highly prejudicial in a jury trial that no steps taken by the judge can prevent the jury from being unduly influenced.

N

Nolo contendere - A Latin phrase that means "I do not contest." A plea of *nolo contendere* has the same effect as a plea of guilty for criminal sentencing but typically may not be considered as an admission of guilt for any other purpose. However, one should never enter such a plea without competent legal counsel and without considering the possible future implications. A previous *nolo* plea could potentially be raised, for example, in a future proceeding to challenge a person's integrity or credibility as a witness.

Nondischargeable debt - A debt that cannot be eliminated in bankruptcy. Examples include a home mortgage, debts for alimony or child support, certain taxes, debts for most government funded or guaranteed educational loans or benefit overpayments, debts arising from death or personal injury caused by driving while intoxicated or under the influence of drugs, and debts for restitution or a criminal fine included in a sentence on the debtor's conviction of a crime. Some debts, such as debts for money or property obtained by false pretenses and debts for fraud or defalcation while acting in a fiduciary capacity may be declared nondischargeable only if a creditor timely files and prevails in a nondischargeability action.

Nonexempt assets - Property of a debtor that can be liquidated to satisfy claims of creditors.

O

Objection - In a trial proceeding if a party asks an improper question or seeks to present evidence the rules do not permit the lawyer for the other party can object to that and ask the court to prevent it. This is called making an objection. The term could also apply to objections to the procedures being followed. In general, objections that are not made right away, at a time when the court can act on them before any harm is done, are deemed to be waived. Lawyers need to be prepared and alert to make sure they object in a proper and timely manner when necessary. On the other hand, clients often feel as though the lawyer should object at times when the lawyer does not for tactical or other reasons. If that happens the lawyer should be able to explain to you why he or she did not object.

Opinion - A judge's written explanation of the decision of the court. The opinion may be that of a single judge or may reflect the collective decision of a panel of judges. When a court that hears appeals decides a case it may be heard by three or more judges. These appellate decisions can take several forms. If all the judges completely agree on the result, one judge will write the opinion for all. If all the judges do not agree, the formal decision will be based upon the view of the majority, and one member of the majority will write the opinion. The judges who did not agree with the majority may write separately in dissenting or concurring opinions to present their views. A dissenting opinion disagrees with the reasoning or the principles of law the majority used to decide the case. A concurring opinion agrees with the decision of the majority opinion, but offers further comment or clarification or even an entirely different reason for reaching the same result. Only the majority opinion can serve as binding precedent in future cases. See also precedent.

Oral argument - An opportunity for lawyers to summarize their position before the court and also to answer the judges' questions.

P

Parole evidence - The term for evidence someone want to offer to explain or add to the written terms of an agreement. Usually such evidence will not be accepted by a court, because the court will feel bound to enforce and interpret the agreement according to its own terms. There are good reasons for this rule. If parties to an agreement could explain it or supplement it by words or documents outside the agreement, the end result could be to make the written agreement meaningless. An exception to this is when the agreement is incomplete, not clear, or ambiguous. When that happens a court may accept evidence about what the parties intended to help clarify the written terms or even in some cases to supplement the written terms when something is not addressed.

Per curiam - Latin, meaning "for the court." In appellate courts, often refers to an unsigned opinion.

Peremptory challenge - In a jury trial one of the first steps is to choose the people who will serve on the jury. In that process of jury selection the parties are allowed to challenge jurors for cause, meaning there is a reason to question whether the person can truly be open minded and objective. In addition to those challenges, parties may have a limited number of peremptory challenges that grant the right to exclude a certain number of prospective jurors without cause or giving a reason.

Petit jury (or trial jury) - A group of citizens who hear the evidence presented by both sides at trial and determine the facts in dispute. Federal criminal juries consist of 12 persons. Federal civil juries consist of at least six persons.

Petition - The document that initiates certain types of legal proceedings, for example bankruptcy proceeding. A bankruptcy petition states basic information regarding the debtor, including name, address, chapter under which the case is filed and estimated amount of assets and liabilities.

Plaintiff - A person or business that files a formal complaint with the court.

Plan - A debtor's detailed description of how the debtor proposes to pay creditors' claims over a fixed period of time.

Plea - In a criminal case, the defendant's statement pleading "guilty" or "not guilty" in answer to the charges. See also *nolo contendere*.

Pleadings - The general term for written statements filed with the court that make a claim, ask for relief, or describe a party's legal or factual assertions about the case. The complaint that starts a suit is a pleading, as is a motion filed with the court. Lawyers have an ethical duty when signing pleadings to do so only when they have a reasonable belief that the pleading is honest and accurate. Some pleadings have to be verified, meaning they are submitted under oath.

Power of attorney - A written instrument under which one person (the principal) authorizes another person or persons (the agent or agents) to act for the principal in financial or legal matters, or regarding health care and medical decisions.

Precedent - A court decision in an earlier case with facts and legal issues similar to a dispute currently before a court. Judges generally must follow precedent from courts having higher authority meaning that they use the principles established in earlier cases to decide new cases that have similar facts and raise similar legal issues. In analyzing issues the judge may determine that a precedent is not really controlling because of differences in the facts or law that applies. Higher level courts may have the ability to review or even overrule their own precedents though the principle of *stare decisis* calls for precedent to be followed in general. (See Common Law).

Preferential debt payment - In bankruptcy cases, all the unsecured creditors are supposed to be treated the same and no creditor should be rewarded for getting paid ahead of the others. The court can nullify a payment made to a creditor in the 90-day period before a debtor files bankruptcy (or within one year if the creditor was an "insider") if the payment gives the creditor more than the creditor would otherwise receive in the debtor's case. The creditor can be required to pay the money back into the court. This makes it very important to be careful in dealing with people or businesses that owe you when their financial circumstances are precarious.

Presentence report - A report prepared after a person has been convicted of a crime summarizing for the court the background information needed to determine the appropriate sentence.

Pretrial conference - A meeting of the judge and lawyers to plan the trial. They discuss the parties' readiness for trial, what issues need to be decided, and in a jury trial which matters should be presented to the jury. The judge and lawyers review proposed evidence and witnesses, and set a trial schedule. Typically, the judge and the parties also discuss the possibility of settlement of the case. By listening to the comments of the judge and other parities litigants can often see the likely outcome of a trial, which in turn helps them evaluate possible settlements.

Priority - In bankruptcy, the Bankruptcy Code's statutory ranking of the order in which unsecured claims will be paid if (as is usual) there is not enough money to pay all unsecured claims in full.

Priority claim - An unsecured claim that is entitled to be paid ahead of other unsecured claims. For example, even without security or a lien, tax liabilities, alimony and child support come ahead of most other claims.

Probation - In criminal cases, with probation, instead of sending an individual to prison, the court releases the person to the community under orders to complete a period of supervision monitored by a probation officer and to abide by certain conditions.

Procedure - The manner of conducting a legal proceeding. In court there are rules for conducting a lawsuit, including rules of civil procedure, criminal procedure, evidence, bankruptcy, and appellate procedure. In other proceedings, such as before government agencies, there will usually be rules of procedure that need to be followed. Although modern legal practice is against technical mistakes causing people to lose their rights, any failure to follow the rules of procedure can still have serious consequences.

Promissory note - As the name implies, a promissory note, or simply note, is a paper by which one person promises to pay money to another. Usually the note will be dated and will say who is going to pay money to whom, when, and with what rate of interest, if any. A note may be paid over a period in regular amounts, say monthly for five years. Sometimes the payments are not all the same, and sometimes the note is payable all at once on a state date (called a date certain). Some notes are payable on demand, meaning the person to whom the money is owed can demand payment at any time but meanwhile the person who has to pay may pay nothing or may just pay interest. Some notes have what is called a balloon feature, meaning that after some number of regular payments the remaining unpaid balance is due all at once in a single payment.

Proof of claim - An official form filed in bankruptcy to set forth the amount of money owed to the creditor by the debtor.

Pro se - Representing oneself instead of hiring an attorney. Serving as one's own lawyer.

Prosecute - To charge someone with a crime. A prosecutor tries a criminal case on behalf of the government. This term can also be used generally in the sense of prosecuting one's legal case. A party's neglect of a case or failure to follow procedure or the obligation to file papers can result in dismissal of the case for non prosecution.

Pro tem - Temporary.

Q

Qualify, qualification - You will often see references to qualifying or qualifications n reference to elective or appointive office. Election or appointment to an office or position is not effective unless the person so chosen is "qualified." Typically, that means among other things being of the required age, such as the requirement in the Constitution that a person be at least 30 to qualify to be elected a Senator. The would be senator must also reside in the state from which the senator will be elected. Another example is qualification for public office of any kind commonly requires taking an oath.

Quid pro quo - Latin for "this for that." It describes an exchange and can simply mean the consideration or payment from one party to another for goods or services. It can be used in reference to sexual harassment in which employment benefits are conditioned on sexual favors.

R

Record - A written account of the doings in a case before a court or a proceeding in front of some other agency or tribunal. This can include recordings of the proceedings, written transcriptions of the proceedings, legal papers filed, applications, documents, and other evidence submitted. Usually the reason such a record is compiled is because there will be an appeal or new proceeding in another court or tribunal to review the proceedings reflected in the record. In some cases, it is very important what is in the record because no new evidence can be submitted later.

Redemption - Action by a debtor to recover property from a secured creditor by paying the amount owed. The debtor may then retain the property. Some laws such a mortgage foreclosure laws on real estate provide debtors a right to redeem the property if they act within a certain time, such as within a year after the foreclosure. These rules are set by state laws and vary from state to state.

Regulation - This can include rules issued by government agencies that enforce the laws enacted by the Congress or a state legislature that need to be elaborated or expanded to work in day to day life. For example, when Congress enacted laws against discrimination in the workplace, it included in the law the creation of an agency to administer the law and gave it the power to make rules and regulations to do that. The agency adopted regulations that give expanded guidance to employers how to comply and that set up procedures for complaints about unlawful discrimination to be received and investigated. A key point about this is that a regulation can carry out or supplement the law that authorizes it, but it cannot change the law or contradict it. If the regulation conflicts with the underlying law or goes beyond what the law authorizes, a court may find the regulation to be invalid.

Remand - Send back.

Res ipsa loquitur - The thing speaks for itself. Used to describe events that could not occur absent fault on the part of someone, thus allowing negligence to be proved without actual evidence of the act or failure to act that was negligent. For example, if an elevator falls and a passenger in it is injured, it might not be necessary to prove any actual negligence to know that elevators are not supposed to fall and thus hold the person controlling the elevator and its operation responsible unless that person can prove something caused the fall that was not that person's fault.

Res judicata - The thing has been decided. A Latin phrase used as a shorthand for the rule that once a party brings a case the court decides the party cannot bring the same case again hoping for a different result.

Reverse - The act of a court setting aside the decision of a lower court. A reversal is often accompanied by a remand to the lower court for further proceedings.

Right - A legally protected interest or freedom, created by the law or by an agreement.

Rule - The term "rule" can be used in a general sense for a legal mandate or principle, or it can be used in a more limited sense for a statement of requirements that has been issued by a government authority (see regulation) or court, such as rules for the procedures before a court.

S

Sanction - A penalty or other type of enforcement used to bring about compliance with the law or with rules and regulations.

Secured creditor - A secured creditor is an individual or business that holds a claim against the debtor that is secured by a lien on property of the estate. The property subject to the lien is the secured creditor's collateral.

Secured debt - Debt backed by a mortgage, pledge of collateral, or other lien; debt for which the creditor has the right to pursue specific pledged property upon default. Examples include home mortgages, auto loans and tax liens.

Sentence - The punishment ordered by a court for a defendant convicted of a crime.

Service of process - The delivery of writs or summonses to the appropriate party.

Settlement - Parties to a lawsuit resolve their dispute without having a trial. Settlements often involve the payment of compensation by one party in at least partial satisfaction of the other party's claims, but usually do not include the admission of fault.

Sequester - To separate. Sometimes juries are sequestered from outside influences during their deliberations.

Standard of proof - Degree of proof required. In criminal cases, prosecutors must prove a defendant's guilt "beyond a reasonable doubt." The majority of civil lawsuits require proof "by a preponderance of the evidence" (50 percent plus), but in some the standard is higher and requires "clear and convincing" proof.

Statute - A law passed by a legislature.

Statute of limitations - The time within which a lawsuit must be filed or a criminal prosecution begun. The deadline can vary, depending on the type of civil case or the crime charged.

Sua sponte - Latin, meaning "of its own will." Often refers to a court taking an action in a case without being asked to do so by either side.

Subordination, subordinate - The act or process by which a person's rights or claims are ranked below those of others.

Subpoena - A command, issued under a court's authority, to a witness to appear and give testimony.

Subpoena duces tecum - A command to a witness to appear and produce documents.

Summary judgment - A decision made on the basis of statements and evidence presented for the record without a trial. It is used when it is not necessary to resolve any factual disputes in the case. Summary judgment is granted when – on the undisputed facts in the record – one party is entitled to judgment as a matter of law.

T

Temporary restraining order - Akin to a preliminary injunction, it is a judge's short-term order forbidding certain actions until a full hearing can be conducted. Often referred to as a TRO.

Testimony - Evidence presented orally by witnesses during trials or before grand juries.

Toll - To suspend or delay, as in the running of the statute of limitations. See statute of limitations.

Tort - A civil, not criminal, wrong. A negligent or intentional injury against a person or property, with the exception of breach of contract.

Trade - Usually refers to the commercial exchange of goods or services. Can also mean an occupation.

Trade mark - Distinctive image, distinctive words, or a combination of the two that identifies a product or service. For example, the words "Pepsi Cola" in the distinctive script of that beverage's name is a trademark (or trade name). A trademark is intended to be associated with the product or service and to trigger recognition and a favorable association in the public mind. For that reason, federal and state intellectual property laws provide for the protection of trademarks so the goodwill associated with them cannot be appropriated by others to promote their businesses.

Trade secret - Information, knowledge, process or technique that is not generally known that gives a business and advantage. For example, the Uniform Trade Secrets Act defines a trade secret as:

- information, including a formula, pattern, compilation, program, device, method, technique, or process,

- that derives independent economic value, actual or potential, from not being generally known to or readily ascertainable through appropriate means by other persons who might obtain economic value from its disclosure or use; and
- is the subject of efforts that are reasonable under the circumstances to maintain its secrecy.

Transcript - A written, word-for-word record of what was said, either in a proceeding such as a trial, or during some other formal conversation, such as a hearing or oral deposition.

Trust - As the name implies, this is a property arrangement in which the owner of property (the grantor) entrusts it to another person or entity (the trustee) who controls the property and uses it for the benefit of another person or to accomplish purposes the owner defined. The beneficiary or beneficiaries of the trust are those for whom the grantor entrusted the property to the trustee. Common examples are trusts created by a parent to hold assets that are transferred (at death or otherwise) for the benefit of children. Because the trustee holds this special relationship of trust to both the grantor and the beneficiary(ies) the trustee is held to a high standard of good faith and responsibility and can be liable for any negligence or misconduct with the trust assets. Trusts are most often created by written trust instruments, but a trust relationship can be created verbally or just by the delivery of the property to the trustee with the terms of the trust understood.

Trustee - The person or entity named in a trust to carry out its terms. In bankruptcy cases, the person appointed by the court to supervise the bankruptcy proceeding.

U

U.S. attorney - A lawyer appointed by the President in each judicial district to prosecute and defend cases for the federal government. The U.S. Attorney employs a staff of Assistant U.S. Attorneys who appear as the government's attorneys in individual cases.

U.S. trustee - An officer of the U.S. Department of Justice responsible for supervising the administration of bankruptcy cases, estates, and trustees; monitoring plans and disclosure statements; monitoring creditors' committees; monitoring fee applications; and performing other statutory duties.

Undersecured claim - A debt secured by property that is worth less than the amount of the debt.

Undue hardship - A term used in zoning cases to describe a hardship caused by the strict application of zoning regulations that practically destroys all beneficial use of real property. If the owner can show such undue hardship, local zoning authorities typically can grant some relief to enable the owner to make a productive use of the property.

Unlawful detainer action - A lawsuit brought by a landlord against a tenant to evict the tenant from rental property – usually for nonpayment of rent.

Unsecured claim - A claim or debt for which a creditor holds no special assurance of payment, such as a mortgage or lien; a debt for which credit was extended based solely upon the creditor's assessment of the debtor's future ability to pay.

Uphold - The appellate court agrees with the lower court decision and allows it to stand. See affirmed.

V

Venue - The geographic area in which a court has jurisdiction. A change of venue is a change or transfer of a case from one judicial district to another.

Verdict - The decision of a trial jury or a judge that determines the guilt or innocence of a criminal defendant, or that determines the final outcome of a civil case.

Voir dire - Jury selection process of questioning prospective jurors, to ascertain their qualifications and determine any bias they may have or other basis for challenge.

W

Wage garnishment - A nonbankruptcy legal proceeding whereby a plaintiff or creditor seeks to subject to his or her claim the future wages of a debtor. In other words, the creditor seeks to have part of the debtor's future wages paid to the creditor for a debt owed to the creditor.

Warrant - Court authorization, most often for law enforcement officers, to conduct a search or make an arrest.

Warranty (warrantee) - A promise about how something will work or perform, or how long it will last. Typically, this term appears with products, machines, equipment, or home construction where the seller of the product "warrants" to the buyer that the product will perform in a certain way for a defined time. Some laws provide for warranties to be "implied" in every transaction, such as that goods that are sold to you conform to the normal standards for those kinds of goods, or are suitable for the normal uses of such goods. Sellers want their exposure to warranty claims to be limited or predictable, so they often try to "disclaim" or modify the warranties by written statements (see Disclaimer). Try really reading the product leaflet that comes with your next appliance, for example, and you probably will find there language aimed at limited how long the manufacturer warrants the product, for what purposes, and whether implied warranties are disclaimed. The law often says that the seller of consumer products cannot disclaim or limit basic warranty protections. This is an area where it can be very important to read carefully and know your rights...

Will - The statement made by a person of who the person wishes to receive his or her property upon the person's death. To be effective the will usually needs to be in writing and needs to be witnessed, typically by two or three witnesses who are not receiving anything from the person. To make a will, a person must be legally an adult and must be mentally sound. Sometimes the law will make a will effective that does not meet all the normal legal formalities, such as a will hand written and signed by the person who made it. Every state makes its own laws on this, though many states have adopted laws aimed at making the law the same among all the states that enact them.

Witness - A witness is a person who sees or hears something and can describe it later. In a lawsuit or other adversary proceeding witnesses give testimony before the court or jury or other decision making body. A witness may also be an expert in a field of knowledge who is allowed to testify about that knowledge. Some documents are also witnessed, such as wills, deeds, promissory notes, and other important documents. The underlying reason is so that the witness or witnesses could, if necessary, come before a court to verify that the document was signed by the person to be bound by it.

Writ - A written court order directing a person to take, or refrain from taking, a certain act.

Writ of certiorari - An order issued by the U.S. Supreme Court directing the lower court to transmit records for a case which it will hear on appeal.

www.ingramcontent.com/pod-product-compliance
Lightning Source LLC
Chambersburg PA
CBHW061445180526
45170CB00004B/1567